COULD YOUR SPOUSE HAVE BORDERLINE PERSONALITY DISORDER?

Understanding the Roses and Rage of BPD

ROBERT PAGE

Book #1 in the *Roses and Rage BPD* Series

For more information, visit the Amazon Author Central for Robert Page at
amazon.com/author/robertpagewriter
or email: robertpagewriter@gmail.com
and join the Facebook support group: Roses and Rage: Spouses of Borderline Personality Disorder

Print version ISBN-13 9781702624251

CONTENTS

INTRODUCTION

"If you leave, I will kill myself RIGHT THIS MINUTE!"

At the time my wife screamed those words at me, I really didn't understand what I was dealing with. Like most spouses of someone with borderline personality disorder, I didn't know I was one. I had to learn the truth of my situation in a long, painful series of baby steps, giant steps, and mostly missteps.

You don't have to suffer the same journey.

This book is a down and dirty "street-guide" to borderline personality disorder (BPD) that assigns names to the demons in your marriage, allowing you the knowledge and power to seek solutions.

A friend, family member, coworker, or therapist—someone in your life has probably already said something like, "You know, maybe you should read about borderline personality disorder and see what you think."

However, most Borderlines refuse to be diagnosed, so you are left to find information on your own, usually in secret.

Not sure what to do, you did some searching on the internet and found the subject eerily familiar, but also overwhelming. So much of the material is written in a very clinical or unrelatable fashion. The authors are usually academic-minded professors (writing for their peers) or memoirs from those with BPD (writing for *their* peers).

What about perspective from one of *your* peers?

I never found any books written before this one *by* a spouse of BPD *for* other spouses of BPD. So, I'm here to distill the information in a way that people like you and I need to hear it—straight talk from someone who's been there.

I'm not trying to get tenure or purge myself of inner turmoil. I just want to help people by writing the kind of book I wish someone had written for me.

Within these pages you'll find a concise, non-clinical overview that says, "Here's what BPD looks like." This will likely be followed by your response of, "That sounds just like life in my home."

I've been there. The wondering, doubting, blaming, shouting, escaping, crying, denying, love-hating, and hate-loving of it all. BPD is a beast of a burden.

Hopefully, you can read these pages and come to a quick conclusion that you're dealing with something other than BPD. If so, that's good news, and I wish you well.

For many of you however, this book will solidify what you've been suspecting for a while now—you are living with a Borderline Personality (or simply, BP).

If you come to that conclusion, don't freak out (okay, a little freaking out is understandable). In addition to what you find in this overview, I've written books with much more information. And there are plenty of other excellent resources available to help, many of which are listed in the back of this book.

I say this often in my BPD writings: *you are not alone.* There are thousands of BPD spouses out there feeling just as crazy and battle-weary as you. Through what can be learned here and elsewhere, we all embolden each other on our path towards a better way.

Okay, let's not get too far ahead of our topic. First, we need to acquire some basic understanding of BPD, then we'll be ready to unpack what the symptoms look like in everyday life.

What Exactly Is Borderline Personality Disorder?
For one thing, BPD belongs to a broader category called "Personality Disorders." Other members of this group include bi-polar personality disorder and narcissistic personality disorder (there are others as well). Some people suffer from more than one of these at a time.

The "bible" used in the psychiatric profession to identify personality disorders is the *Diagnostic and Statistical Manual.* It receives occasional updates, and the editions we will draw from are the fourth and fifth.

The *DSM-IV* lists nine symptoms of BPD in dry but mostly comprehensible language. It states that clinicians should determine that at least five of the symptoms are present before a diagnosis can be made. That's surprisingly simple for the layperson to understand—so of course they had to muck it up.

The *DSM-5* (I have no idea why they switched from Roman numerals to Arabic), attempts to "improve" the list of symptoms, with mixed results. It gives clinicians more freedom to diagnose without the "5 of 9" mandate, but it also makes it much harder for people on the street to use.

With that bit of background out of the way, the main description from the *DSM-IV* tells us that BPD is:

> *A pervasive pattern of instability of interpersonal relationships, self-image, and affects, and marked impulsivity beginning by early adulthood and present in a variety of contexts.*

Like I mentioned; the language is clinical. Let's run it through a real-world filter.

I would focus on the keywords "pervasive" and "variety." If the various symptoms listed between those two words aren't happening regularly and in lots of different places, we're not talking about BPD.

Makes sense, right? All of us have *some* BPD-like symptoms *some* of the time. Feeling occasionally unstable and impulsive hardly rates notice.

Fears of being alone or wondering if your spouse is having an affair are not outside the range of "normal." But a Borderline presents these symptoms (and several others) in regular and extreme patterns.

The bulk of this book will address the specifics of these various symptoms, including how to spot them in your daily life.

For now, it's enough to know that BPD is a disorder of the personality and that the symptoms are ongoing and present in a variety of situations. Got it? Then let's move on.

The Layout of This Book

Each chapter addresses a prominent symptom and the heading comes from a relevant song title.

After unpacking the "clinical" definition, the symptom is viewed as a spouse of BPD is likely to see it in day-to-day homelife. It's not always pretty, and I expect there will be times you call out loud, "Holy crap! That's exactly what happened to me!"

Like I said, you are not alone.

Keep in mind, it is not typical that a BP will present *all* the possible symptoms. Some symptoms may come and go while others will never appear at all. I know it's tempting, but try not to look at the list of symptoms like a scoresheet.

After we walk through all the symptoms together, I offer resources to you as needed. The overview found here might be all you need, but if you want more insight, I can help you with that in my expanded book, *BPD from the Husband's POV: The Roses and Rage of My Wife's Borderline Personality Disorder*. It's loaded with real-life (and sometimes cringe-inducing) experiences to help you navigate through your own marriage.

A Warning

I am not a clinical psychologist or marriage counselor. I am not here to diagnose your spouse. In fact, many BPs never get officially diagnosed because they refuse to consider the possibility. But formal diagnosis is not the point.

It's not about hanging a label on your wife or husband that says, "I told you it was all your fault!" At most, you'll likely just have to be content knowing your spouse has many of the traits associated with BPD. Giving the problem a name is incredibly helpful. That is enough for you to initiate a quest for improvements instead of assigning blame.

A Quick Note About "They," "Them," and "Their"

In order to be gender inclusive and avoid clumsy s/he variations, I'm choosing to use the words "they," "them," and "their" in singular form where needed.

Now, if you're ready to tackle the list of BPD symptoms and compare them to what you see in your marriage, turn the page and dive in. Be prepared—it might get messy.

IF YOU LEAVE ME NOW

Abandonment: intense, unstable, and conflicted close relationships, marked by mistrust, neediness, and anxious preoccupation with real or imagined abandonment (*DSM-5*).

The National Institute of Mental Health adds:

> *BPDs may display efforts to avoid real or imagined abandonment, such as rapidly initiating intimate (physical or emotional) relationships or cutting off communication with someone in anticipation of being abandoned.*

The scariest part for the BPD spouse with regards to the above descriptions is "real or imagined." If the BP is in a full-on, fight or flight abandonment rage, you are basically screwed no matter what you do.

If you actually committed an act to trigger the event—screwed.

If you actually committed no act whatsoever—yup, still screwed.

For the former, the reaction you face from your spouse will be *far* more intense than what you feel is appropriate. You'll think, "Fine. I did something questionable, but does it really mean the world is ending?"

For the later, you'll be swamped defending yourself against preposterous accusations and think, "Where the heck is all this coming from?"

Good question. Let's talk about why abandonment is such an enormous issue for the BP.

In *I Hate You—Don't Leave Me: Understanding the Borderline Personality*, authors Jerold Kreisman and Hal Straus say this about abandonment as perceived by the BP:

> *Just as an infant cannot distinguish between the temporary absence of her mother and her 'extinction,' the borderline often experiences temporary aloneness as perpetual isolations.*

In the grips of despair, they add that the BP becomes "enraged at the world (or whoever is handy) for depriving her of this basic fulfillment."

At this point, you might be asking, "So, even though my spouse is an adult, you're telling me they are responding to abandonment like a baby?"

Yup. That's about it. It's all wrapped up in the unstable self-image most BPs have that we'll talk about in later chapters. You and I long ago developed the tools to understand and cope with feeling alone and knowing it's a temporary condition. The loved one who just walked out the door is still "there," just not "here." We miss them but don't assume their total demise.

The BP doesn't have that same confidence. They become convinced that your absence is proof-positive you will never return. And because they rely on you to boost their unstable sense of self, your absence threatens their own existence. If you don't exist, neither do they.

Just as mentioned above, a BP's fear converts into an attack on "whoever is handy" without regard to reasonable facts. And guess what? The handy person is *you*, because as a spouse, you are always the most available target.

What Abandonment Symptoms Look Like in Daily Life
You have spent your whole life slowly developing a sense of what behaviors are considered "normal" during regular interaction with your loved ones. You feel quite confident you have those basics figured out.

Then you married a BP and your perceptions crash down in a blizzard of glass shards. Confronted by a flash of white-hot anger, you're suddenly defending yourself for actions that until then were solidly mundane and unnoteworthy.

That's a glimpse of what crossing the abandonment line with a BP looks like. The BP might feel ashamed of their behavior later, but in the heat of the moment, there is no containment.

In my marriage to Lyssa (not her real name), symptoms of abandonment issues appeared immediately after arriving at home from our honeymoon. Feeling tired, I moved towards the bedroom. She abruptly asked, "But if you take a nap, what am I going to do?"

Her question hardly registered with me at the time. In my mind, I was only talking about a short nap because I was worn out from our recent travels. But to her BPD mind, her new husband was "leaving her alone," which she quickly amplified into, "he doesn't really love me or he'd know how this makes me feel."

It was a short leap for her to then mutate that fear into an accusative question put to me, as if I was somehow misbehaving. This was only the first of many examples of the "if you leave me now" fears she brought into our marriage.

After the pace of our marital disagreements increased, Lyssa made me promise I would never walk out on her during an argument. This seemed reasonable at the time. Adults should be able to work things out if they care for each other. The key word being "adults," and as I found out much later, BPs are emotional children in grown up bodies.

Unfortunately, she was not attempting to make improvements to our interpersonal communications skills. Lyssa's BPD was simply deploying landmines to keep me from triggering her fears of abandonment. Now, if I did leave in the midst of a fight, she could toss, "LIAR!" onto the pile of accusations. All of her previous false accusations then become justified.

Lyssa's fear of abandonment escalated over the years to include:

--blocking doorways to keep me trapped in a room
--taking my car keys

--extensive verbal abuse in the form of insults and beratement
--threating to commit suicide (several times)
--jumping on the hood of my car while I was driving out of a parking lot

In *Stop Walking on Eggshells: Taking Your Life Back When Someone You Care About Has Borderline Personality Disorder*, authors Paul Mason and Randi Kreger quote a BP named Tess who says:

> *When I feel abandoned, I feel a combination of isolation, terror, and alienation. I panic. I feel betrayed and used. I think I'm going to die.*

Are you starting to appreciate the seriousness of this symptom in the life of a BP? Your simple act of "going out with some friends" hits the BP like a pronouncement of final doom. There is no grey area for them. Your spouse does not have the ability to be "a little" distraught about abandonment.

A non-BP (the term we'll use to describe anyone whose life is negatively affected by the actions of a BP) will face an onslaught of guilt and self-doubt as they defend against a seemingly unprovoked attack.

Or, the non-BP may get caught up in the emotional level of the BP, meeting the severity of the attack with a proportional response. This can easily lead to domestic abuse and physical injury.

After all my personal experience and study, I believe that fear of abandonment is the prime symptom among all the others a BP may present. In other words, if the BP in your life begins spinning out of control and turning against you, more often than not you are witnessing an extreme expression of "don't leave me" even if they say it's about something else.

Other symptoms may also be at play, but fear of abandonment is the one fueling them all.

The importance of understanding the abandonment symptom is why this chapter is the longest in the book. The other symptoms are still very important, but won't require as much time to review.

For a deeper look at the all-or-nothing view of the BP, read on...

ALL OR NOTHING AT ALL

Extremes: close relationships often viewed in extremes of idealization and devaluation and alternating between over involvement and withdrawal (*DSM-5*).

Here's what the National Institute of Mental Health has to say about the symptom of extremes:

> *BPDs tend to view things in extremes, such as all good or all bad, and their opinions of other people can also change quickly, leading to intense and unstable relationships.*

A component of the BP's extreme worldview is called "splitting" and it's crucial you understand what this is about.

Splitting

The act of a BP swinging wildly between idolizing and demonizing a person is called splitting. The BP will likely base their feelings about you on the most current interaction the two of you have had. All your previous interactions don't count as much as the current moment.

While most people have the ability to cope with contradictions and grey areas, a BP sees only good or evil and has no memory of previously assigning one label to another person while in the clutch of the polar opposite. The BP exists in an *all-or-nothing* world.

It is helpful to know what this symptom looks like from the non-clinical viewpoint of a Borderline. In an article from *The Mighty* blog (link available in the back of the book), a contributor named Stacey writes:

> *I rage so hard at the people I love most but I'm also desperate for them to not leave. I know I'm 'a lot' when I have such a passionate love/hate thing going on, but it's a package deal.*

I hear Stacey saying that she can't help the way she acts any more than you can change the color of your eyes. Maybe she'd change if she could, but for now that's just the way it is.

What Extreme/Splitting Symptoms Look Like in Daily Life
One moment you're enjoying a funny Netflix movie with your spouse, chuckling lightly over the actions of the characters. A moment later you're under verbal attack for being thoughtless and without morals. Your spouse demands that you must apologize right this instant!

What happened to your pleasant movie night? I'll tell you—your spouse's BPD kicked in when you were looking the other way.

Back up a few moments and recall what was on the screen. I can guarantee you there was something that triggered your spouse's fear of abandonment: a sexual suggestion, a dirty joke, a love scene—something.

You didn't notice it, but that's when your spouse zeroed in on your reaction. They think that since you didn't turn away you must approve of "that smut" on the screen. There is *no* middle ground. The *only* conclusion is that you will leave your spouse to pursue a depraved life elsewhere.

Rather than take a breath and realize they are letting their imagination get *way* ahead, your spouse simply attacks. All your previous loving actions count for nothing. The only thing that matters is the absolute horror your spouse feels at the thought of you not being the angel they believed. You have betrayed them.

Since you can't be viewed as "mostly an angel," the only choice is to fully demonize you. All or nothing. Your spouse is disgusted at the thought of being married to someone so unworthy.

In the shock of this surprise attack, you flail about trying to defend yourself, but everything you say makes them more upset. That's because they aren't mad about the thing they say they are mad about (something in the movie).

Instead, they are terrified you'll be leaving them alone to face their own fear of existence. But explaining to you they feel that way might sound "crazy" which would also make you want to leave, so they keep attacking instead.

It can take hours or days, but eventually your spouse sees actions from you that earn your promotion back to "angel" status and life is grand. In the meantime, your head is still spinning as you try to keep up.

♦ ♦ ♦

The concept of splitting ties directly into the BPD symptom, extreme mood swings, which we'll look at next.

BAD MOON RISING

Mood Swings: unstable emotional experiences and frequent mood changes; emotions that are easily aroused, intense, and/or out of proportion to events and circumstances (*DSM-5*).

The NIMH adds the following to our understanding of this symptom:

> BPDs may display intense and highly changeable moods, with each episode lasting from a few hours to a few days, along with uncertainty about how they see themselves and their role in the world.

You may be noticing by now that some BPD symptoms overlap. This is certainly true of a BP's tendency to view the world in extremes and have mood swings.

While it is possible for a BP to also be bi-polar, the two are not the same. It is generally believed that the mood swings of a BP are more intense and tend to shift between extremes faster.

One of the most striking aspects of mood swings I saw in my marriage was how out of proportion they were to the triggering event.

In my previous experiences with disagreements, two people would gradually increase the level of agitation—confirming and reconfirming several times that their perceptions are correct before a truly elevated conflict is allowed to begin.

With a BP, you will receive no warning shots across the bow. You will move swiftly from calm to calamity. The transition is a tall step, not a smooth ramp.

I used to question my wife Lyssa about why she seemed to skip over several peaceful options and jump straight to full combat mode. Her reply: "Once I make up my mind, there's no reason to wait."

The problem of course, was that her decision to act was based on irrational fears and denial of basic facts. That's a sadly difficult place for the non-BP to find any ground for compromise.

What Mood Swings Look Like in Daily Life

The authors of *Stop Walking on Eggshells* describe that the mood of a BP "may swing from intense anger to depression, depression to irritability, and irritability to anxiety within a few hours." They add, "Non-BPs often find this unpredictability exhausting."

Exhausting is right. There were several nights Lyssa subjected me to sleep deprivation by ripping the bedding and sheets away from me, turning on all the lights in the house, yanking pillows from under my head, and insisting that I engage her in an argument.

The outcome? I would get mad and stay that way for days, while her mood would quickly swing back to pleasant. It was as if my eventual intense response allowed her to relax. The next day, she would criticize me for still being angry and insist on an apology. Yup. I owed *her* an apology.

Mood swings are one of the most difficult challenges when married to a BP. Everything becomes so unpredictable. Eventually, rather than continue breaking social events and commitments, you simply stop making plans with others. You become more isolated and trapped in the world of borderline personality disorder.

◆ ◆ ◆

You may wonder if a BP feels love and relationships the same way you do. To learn more about that very topic, keep reading.

CRAZY LITTLE THING CALLED LOVE

Unstable Relationships: Fears of rejection by – and/or separation from – significant others, associated with fears of excessive dependency and complete loss of autonomy (*DSM-5*).

> *BPDs may display a pattern of intense and unstable relationships with family, friends, and loved ones, often swinging from extreme closeness and love (idealization) to extreme dislike or anger (devaluation).*

People with BPD are prone to enter quickly into romantic relationships. As is their wont, they initially view a new suitor as an angel of delight. They see only the good and surely in this person, they will find all the love they seek.

Merri Lisa Johnson, in *Girl in Need of a Tourniquet: Memoir of a Borderline Personality*, describes her codependence and need for love this way:

> *I need to hear the words. "You win the prize. I will love you forever. You are worth losing everything else." Jackpot. Home base. An umpire whispers in my ear, "You're safe."*

Yet, in a twist of self destruction, the BP will often crash and burn a relationship only to try and start it again. If their partner puts up with it, the cycle of on-and-off-again will continue with great dramatic affect.

In a marriage, ceasing the relationship is arduous to say the least. Instead, the BP tends to create considerable havoc within a household because the tensions are not released through absence. Perhaps you've heard the expression, "fighting like two cats in a bag?"

Although most of the instability occurs between the BP and spouse, other family members are often drawn in. The relationship between a BP and their parents is particularly stormy territory.

With my wife Lyssa, she often engaged in heated arguments with her father. Eventually, she stripped him of his role as "dad" and would only refer to him by his first name.

As our marriage progressed, she soon transferred her feelings towards her father to me. I became the narcissistic control freak who never listened. She would scream, "How did this happen to me again?" She never wanted a real answer.

What Unstable Relationships Look Like in Daily Life
Look for signs of idealization and devaluation in your marriage. Does your spouse adore you as the "world's best lover" only to chastise you the next day as a conniving cheat? You will be seen as a savior one moment and a devil the next. Here's a real-world example.

While my wife and I watched the *Simpsons*, I chuckled at a scene in which Marge gets caught outside in the nude and zips around the neighborhood to find cover. What came next was a blowup that lasted all night and into the next day.

What happened? She split me. Her BP mind was not able to consider that a naked body in a TV show was not porn, even if that body (a cartoon body at that) was not literally shown onscreen or in a sexual nature. Porn is porn.

Furthermore, if her husband sees a porn object, he *must* want to have sex with it, which means he will find someone else more attractive than her and leave. This will happen because he is clearly a vile, disgusting creature capable of only horrid actions. Her solution to this lightning-fast conclusion was to attack me first before I committed the crime she imagined me plotting.

Apparently, a chuckle is not just a chuckle.

◆ ◆ ◆

I hope you're intrigued by this book to this point. If so, **I have a favor to ask...**

PASS IT ON

If you're finding this "short-read" book useful, I'd be very grateful if you'd **post an honest review** with Amazon. The more reviews, the higher the chances others who need the book will see it.

To leave a review, all you need to do is visit the book's Amazon page. Scroll down to see a button/link that says "Write a customer review" – click on that and you're good to go. While you're at the page, please "follow" me as an author so you'll be notified about future books.

Thank you for the support,
~Robert

In the eBook, you may click/tap here to leave a review.

Tell Me Your Story!
I love to hear from readers. Join the Facebook support group, Roses and Rage: Spouses of Borderline Personality Disorder, to share your experiences. I would especially love to hear from spouses who have found ways to reduce the BPD problems in your relationship.

Now, let's continue with the symptom of distorted self-image...

CAUGHT IN THE MIDDLE

Distorted Self-Image: markedly impoverished, poorly developed, or unstable self-image (*DSM-5*).

The symptom of distorted self-image relates to our earlier discussion of abandonment. By the time you and I reached our young-adult years, we had a strong sense of "who we are." Our core principles and maxims about life were basically in place to direct our choices and actions.

For reasons that are unclear, the BP doesn't develop in the same way. Their self-image stopped forming before it was able to fully take hold.

I know this is difficult for a non-BP to grasp, but try to consider how terrifying it must feel to not be sure that you exist except for how others see you. Take away "others" and what happens to a BP? *Poof!* They see themselves as obliterated.

Without a stable sense of self, they turn to strong figures in their immediate surroundings to provide them meaning. You, as the spouse, are the most likely choice.

At first, you see this as a form of flattery. You are a hero who can do no wrong. You are needed in all ways to provide safety and comfort. Your spouse repeatedly declares, "I'd be lost without you." That's no lie.

But with the passing of time, your spouse's adoration mutates toward a less-attractive neediness. Accusative questions become commonplace:

--"Where are you going?"

--"Why can't you stay home?"

--"Why don't you want anyone to see us together?"

--"Who else will be there?"

--"Why do you always want to spend time with them instead of me?"

Next, neediness transitions to obsession and doing anything apart becomes a battle royal (unless it's their idea—then it's perfectly acceptable).

Your BP spouse becomes trapped in a middle ground where they have no self-image of their own, yet the one co-opted from you is constantly under threat by unwarranted perceptions of your abandonment. The BP is left drifting in the empty space, desperately clinging to personality flotsam for support.

In an article from *The Mighty* blog, a BP contributor named Sarah tries to describe the pain of uncertainty:

> *Being caught between the expectations of others, the expectations I place on myself, the hurt of the past and the fear of the future and the emptiness I feel inside all the time that perpetuates the hopelessness of making it out (of BPD) alive.*

As hard as this situation is for you as the non-BP, you have the potential to take a time-out now and then. Imagine the dread that consumes the BP who lives in their troubled brain 24/7. Their only relief is dependent on you. And when you aren't available at the moment you're needed; the bottom drops out.

What a Distorted Sense of Self Look Like in Daily Life

According to *Stop Walking on Eggshells*, a BP experiencing this symptom will feel the following:

--There is "nothing to me"

--They are different people depending on who they are with

--Being alone leaves them without a sense of self

--They are dependent on others for cues about how to behave, what to think, and how to be

Because the BP is adept at co-opting the best elements of someone else's self-image, the BP is often viewed as very likeable and fun to be around. After all, who wouldn't want to be around a positive version of themselves?

The challenge for the non-BP spouse becomes eventually trying to convince others of what you face in your private marriage. They see your spouse as healthy and happy, and you come along with a story of desperation and rage. Can you blame them for raising an eyebrow of suspicion?

Many BP spouses learn to keep their anguish to themselves and become all the more isolated as the borderline personality disorder continues to shadow everything in their life.

Do you ever wish you could completely let go of inhibitions and be totally crazy and wild? BPs are known for doing that very thing more than most, so we'll talk about that in the next chapter.

DON'T FEAR THE REAPER

Impulsive Behaviors: acting on the spur of the moment in response to immediate stimuli; acting on a momentary basis without a plan or consideration of outcomes (*DSM-5*).

The NIMH lists what some of these activities look like:

> *Impulsive and often dangerous behaviors, such as spending sprees, unsafe sex, substance abuse, reckless driving, and binge eating*

It should be easy for you to imagine those actions being highly destructive to a relationship.

How would you react if you found your husband had smashed yet another car or drained the savings account on a gambling spree? What if your wife maxed out a credit card you didn't even know about or told you she's pregnant by another man and it's your fault for not being a better husband?

The impulsive behavior of a BP can be devastating for the loved ones caught in the wake.

In a blog article at *The Mighty*, a contributor named Sarah deftly describes her impulsive tendencies:

> *There's two sides to you — one that knows you should control your urges and 'behave' as you should; the other that rages against what 'should be' from inside, like poison speeding through your body, bending you to its will, desperate for satisfaction, but no amount of indulging ever truly satiates it.*

For the BP caught up in this symptom, there is no before or after, only now, and the now is often distressing. With less ability to view the before and after (in other words, *consequences*), a BP is much more likely than you are to say, "I want more!"

To make matters even worse, after the BP comes down from the high of their impulsive actions, they tend to underrate the gravity of what happened. While you're left to mop up a catastrophic mess, your spouse is saying, "I don't know what the big deal is."

What Impulsive Behaviors Look Like in Daily Life

When you first meet a BP, you're likely in for a wild but thrilling ride. Activities early in your relationship might include nights on the town, flowing alcohol, recreational drugs, raunchy great sex, and nasty hangovers.

If your new friend is single, you'll be dragging yourself to the toilet while they are already talking about where the next party is that night.

If they are married or in a committed relationship, you were the temporary escape they needed to play out their insatiable need to feel alive, especially to compensate for their lack of self-identity.

If you are married *to* this thrill-seeking BP, you are up all night calling hospitals, texting friends, desperately hoping they are okay, and yet again swearing you won't put up with this bullshit anymore. (side note: you will, many more times).

In my own marriage, my wife used her impulsiveness as a test of my love for her. Sometimes these tests proved to be quite expensive.

One time, she announced that she needed to move out for a while so that "we could both do some thinking." I must admit I didn't hate the idea of putting some space between us. I thought it would help.

We found her a studio rental, paid three times the rent to get her moved in, and bought all the necessities to set up her life there. Six weeks later she was ready to move back. "You never came over to try and win me back," she protested.

♦ ♦ ♦

Another method BPs use to cope with stress and feel alive is to engage in self-harm. To learn more about that, keep reading.

HURT

Self-harm: engagement in dangerous, risky, and potentially self-damaging activities, unnecessarily and without regard to consequences; lack of concern for one's limitations and denial of the reality of personal danger (*DSM-5*).

At first glance this looks similar to the symptom of impulsiveness we just discussed. The difference is that those were actions that *might* cause physical harm while now we're talking about actions *designed* to cause harm. Indeed, harm is inevitable.

The types of self-harm associated with BP behavior may include:

--cutting
--skin scratching
--head banging
--hair pulling
--tearing off scabs
--needle poking
--burning
--biting
--breaking bones

So, why would a BP choose to hurt themselves? Firstly, it's a coping mechanism. If a BP feels numb without a self-identity, pain is a method to feel alive or "real."

In her memoir, *Girl in Need of a Tourniquet*, Merri Lisa Johnson disturbingly describes her self-harm as a message of self-loathing:

> *I want to tell them I carve scarlet letters in my skin like hate mail in the dead letter office of my body.*

BPs often feel no strong connection to their past or future. They are drawn to living in the now, but without a strong sense of self, even the now can feel miserable. The BP wallows in an overwhelming sense of emptiness.

Self-harm, like cutting for example, gives the now meaning. For a shining instant, there is a vivid sensation of feeling alive and purposeful. It may be fleeting, but the rush is enough to keep the BP coming back for more.

Secondly, self-harm sends out non-verbal signals that they need help. I saw examples of this in my marriage.

I often wondered how an intelligent woman like my wife Lyssa could engage in self-harm without having to admit something was terribly wrong with her emotions. But she seemed to do it in a way that was either impulsive or unconscious and therefore "not of her own doing."

She intellectually knew she was engaging in self-harm, but disowned herself of the responsibility. BPs are masters at avoiding consequences. But as her self-harm became undeniable, it led to us seeking therapy.

What Self-Harm Looks Like in Daily Life

With Lyssa, examples of self-harm started with picking at her thumb cuticles. They would often be raw and she'd cover them with bandages. If I asked how they got that way, she dismissed the question as if she actually wasn't sure.

Then, the problem escalated to small cuts on her arms. She never had an explanation. Her answer was always, "Oh, that. I'm not sure how that happened." I never caught her cutting herself, so I couldn't say much about it.

However, on another occasion, she allowed me to witness the entirety of an absolutely brutal example of self-harm.

We had a terrible fight that began with her insisting I never watch movies when she was not home (because I might see a sexual scene and "porn is porn" to a BP). I told her that "was nuts" and refused. She exploded into a rage and launched various accusations at me about not loving her.

At the height of her anger, she demanded that I apologize and comfort her. I fired back, "You got yourself this mad, you can get yourself calm again." She looked around the room as if she was searching for something to hurt me with.

Instead, she ran full speed at the wall and lowered her head just as she hit. She stumbled back, lowered her head, and did it again even harder. This time she collapsed to the floor and cried, "See what you made me do."

This is what being married to a BP looked like for me. There were many vivid and awful moments that will never be forgotten. I try to remind myself that as dreadful as I felt when it was happening, my wife was the true victim. The depth of her pain was beyond my understanding.

♦ ♦ ♦

The ultimate form of self-harm is suicide, but because of its importance and potential finality, we'll address it separately in the next chapter.

SOUND OF SILENCE

Suicide: frequent feelings of being down, miserable, and/or hopeless; difficulty recovering from such moods; pessimism about the future; pervasive shame; feeling of inferior self-worth; thoughts of suicide and suicidal behavior (*DSM-5*).

Of all the BPD traits I faced with my wife Lyssa, suicidal threats were the scariest. I had no training or experience with what I was confronted by and failed miserably at being helpful. Maybe I can help others avoid similar mistakes by sharing what I learned.

An often quoted and terrible statistic is that 8-10 percent of people with borderline personality disorder commit suicide. That's not *attempting* suicide, but actually succeeding.

As high as that number sounds, it might in reality be much higher because it only includes people who were previously diagnosed with BPD. Thousands more go undiagnosed and suicides from their numbers go uncounted as BPD-related.

To some desperate BPs, suicide is the decisive solution to mood swings and depression. A BP would never again have to experience the fear of being left alone to face their own lack of self. In one blazing moment of feeling alive, all their problems are removed.

Attempted suicide is also an excellent method to attract attention. No matter how many arguments a marriage might face, when a BP tries to end it all, the spouse will normally rush to offer compassion and support. It's a game changer to be sure. Or at least it should be.

From the very first instance of suicidal behavior in my marriage, I should have reached out for help. Or at the very least, I should have expressed to Lyssa in a calm moment that any future mention of suicide would result in an emergency 911 call. No exceptions.

According to the National Institute of Mental Health, the spouse of a BP should:

> *Take seriously any comments about suicide or wishing to die. Even if you do not believe your family member or friend will attempt suicide, the person is clearly in distress and can benefit from your help in finding treatment.*

Help can be found by calling the National Suicide Prevention Lifeline toll-free at 1–800–273–TALK (8255), 24 hours a day, 7 days a week. The deaf and hard of hearing can contact the lifeline via TTY at 1–800–799–4889. All calls are free and confidential.

What Threat of Suicide Look Like in Daily Life

I faced four episodes of suicidal behavior with Lyssa. There might have been more I never knew about, but I faced four more than I knew how to handle.

The first episode climaxed with her locking herself in our bathroom and yelling at me about taking a handful of pills. I didn't think we had anything deadly in our supplies, but I couldn't be sure and she wouldn't let me in.

I responded by assuming she was lying and just "acting out" for attention. Who wants to think their spouse is so messed up that they would take their own life? That's what crazy people do, right? And I wasn't married to someone like that. Was I?

The second suicidal event occurred in the midst of a rage when she yelled out, "The only reason I'm not killing myself right now is the thought of what it would do to my little sister."

The amount of pain someone must feel to commit suicide terrifies me. I didn't want to think I could have anything to do with causing such anguish. Therefore, I (borrowing from a BP symptom) dissociated from the moment. I rationalized that she hadn't actually threatened suicide. If anything, she expressed an anti-suicidal statement. Yeah, that's what I told myself.

The third suicidal event came quite a bit later during our 4th year of marriage. In my attempt to leave during one of her rages, she screamed at me in a public setting that if I left, she would kill herself that very minute.

Unlike the previous threats, I actually considered this one believable. Her tone of desperation was at an all-new level. It stopped me in my tracks, and I didn't leave. This time, we sought help, although we did it under the guise of "marriage counseling" rather than admit she had a deeper problem.

Ironically, it was counseling that led to Lyssa's fourth suicidal event.

After several of these counseling sessions, she would become enflamed at me for sharing negative descriptions of our marriage. Remember, a BP doesn't accept shades of gray. If I insult any part of our union, she interprets this as a statement that I don't love anything about us and am looking for a way out the door.

Once, as we walked to the car, she had a complete breakdown and announced that she would be left with no choice but to kill herself if I didn't find a way to make her life better. Oh, that I could have Lyssa. It simply wasn't in my power.

To reiterate, at least 8-10 percent of all BPs commit suicide, probably more. I'm fortunate I didn't lose Lyssa in those days. One rash act and there would have been no do-overs. Her crushing fears of non-existence would have ultimately come true.

UNDER PRESSURE

Anger: persistent or frequent angry feelings; anger or irritability in response to minor slights and insults (*DSM-5*).

After reading this far, you've seen numerous examples of BP anger. If you're married to a BP, you are quite familiar with the concept of unpredictable and seemingly inconsolable rage. It is an awesome spectacle to behold, and terrible to be on the receiving end of.

Anger is particularly dangerous for the non-BP if you are the victim of physical abuse. During a BP rage, it is not unusual for property to be damaged and people to be injured.

As noted by the *DSM-5*, a notable trait of anger in a BP is how it seems to be in response to "minor" slights and insults. As seen with other BPD symptoms, you may witness a jump from one emotional extreme to another in a matter of seconds. There is no "ramping up," but rather an immediate leap from a state of relative calm to that of blind rage. And as a spouse, the focus is usually straight at you.

Merri Lisa Johnson, in her memoir *Girl in Need of a Tourniquet*, brilliantly offers this stark description of BPD anger:

> *Our rage is perverse. Like a strange child, the rage walks backwards. Sarcasm takes scattered steps in a zigzag towards the beloved...High-pitched shrieks followed by the sound of air entering a slit throat is borderline for PLEASE STAY.*

When confronted by anger of this level, most non-BPs will react in two ways—defensively or by leaving—both of which only provoke the BP into deeper anguish. It's a vicious cycle with no winners.

What Anger (Rage) Looks Like in Daily Life

Here is a list I can think of off the top of my head of events that sparked off-the-hook anger in my marriage. I'm talking hours-long rage fests:

--I laughed at a joke on the *Simpsons*
--I won at Scrabble when the app didn't score us correctly
--I asked a stranger (of the opposite sex) for directions
--I high-fived someone (of the opposite sex)
--I applauded at a music performance (an opposite sex drummer)
--I played music while she got ready for us to go out
--I didn't look away from a Victoria's Secret commercial on TV
--I looked away from a Victoria's Secret commercial on TV in a way that made fun of the fact that she insisted I look away

Some of these events make me grin in retrospect. They are rather humorous when looked at as a group. But if you're married to a BP, you can attest that there is nothing funny about the anger when it's happening.

Along the way, there were fist holes put through doors, shattered glass lamps, piles of broken CDs, personal letters destroyed, computer documents altered, friends "unfriended," emails sent falsely representing me, and one time she even caved in an entire kitchen wall.

During the "morning after" these rage attacks, she would hardly acknowledge anything had happened. I would remain fuming for days because of her starting fights over "nothing," and she would glibly say, "You need to learn how to let go."

Nope, a BP isn't big on facing consequences, and being married to a BP ain't for sissies.

♦ ♦ ♦

Part of my spouse's post-anger behavior concerns the symptom of dissociation. Keep reading to see if that's happening in your marriage as well.

IT WASN'T ME

Dissociation: transient, stress-related paranoid ideation or severe dissociative symptoms (*DSM-IV*).

Dissociation is our last primary BPD symptom, and probably the most esoteric for the non-BP to understand. The National Alliance on Mental Illness describes it this way:

> *Disconnecting from your thoughts or sense of identity, or "out of body" type of feelings — and stress-related paranoid thoughts. Severe cases of stress can also lead to brief psychotic episodes.*

To simplify, if the BP experiences symptoms and stress too intense for their psyche to handle, they simply shut down and check out for a while. Like an engine protecting itself from overheating, the system shifts into "safety mode" until the threat diminishes.

Sarah, contributing to an article at *The Mighty* blog, writes:

> *When everything becomes too much, it's like floating into an abyss inside your head; it's darker, and a little fuzzy, but it's warm, and welcoming, and you feel safe in there.*

Talking to a BP in this state is incredibly confusing for a spouse. Attempts to address recent conflicts or bad behavior are met with blank stares or even complete denial. The BP can, at least temporarily, rewrite their history to conveniently omit the negative bits.

To you and me, it appears that the BP is flagrantly lying. We ask ourselves, "How could they *not* remember the awful things that were said and done?" Surely, the BP is playing a game, right?

No. Dissociation is not a ruse meant to consciously dodge responsibility (although a BP will do that too). It's quite likely they just can't focus on the details clearly enough to feel confident about the facts. This is occurring on a subconscious level.

Remember, a married BP usually walks and talks like a completely normal person. But on the inside, they are not well. The word *disorder* is in the name of their ailment for a reason. Sometimes their brains just cannot make the connections that would make life easier.

What Dissociation Looks Like in Daily Life

Sometimes I would say something to my spouse like, "I'm going to change the way I do things because of how you've been treating me." In response, she would look at me with zero comprehension. It's like she thought I must have been talking about someone else.

Here's an example. After we had been married a few years, I noticed several of my precious pre-marital keepsakes had disappeared. My spouse denied any responsibility, but I held firm and insisted her acts of thievery were completely unacceptable. I essentially went on strike and refused any interaction with her until my possessions were returned.

After a couple days, she came into the house and presented me with a large sack. She had stolen far more than I was aware of. While handing me the evidence of her crimes, she insinuated she wasn't sure how she came across it.

She wanted me to believe that the bag had simply "shown up" and that I should reward her for its return. Inconceivably, she expected me to *thank* her for "finding" all my stuff.

The truth was unpleasant, so dissociation rescued her from the responsibility.

♦ ♦ ♦

A Predictable Cycle

Do you see how the symptoms of BPD all interact and support each other? Extremes, anger, and mood swings are often activated simultaneously by an irrational fear of abandonment. Then impulsiveness, self-harm, and dissociation kick in to release the stress. Given a little time, the process starts over again.

In my marriage, I saw a symptom-cycle that lasted about four days. I could mark the calendar and plan for the next emotional eruption. I would go so far as to plan social events around those dates. A friend would invite us to attend a gathering and after consulting the calendar I'd have to say, "We have already have plans that night." Sure enough, the plans would take place as predicted—filled with rage and ruin.

◆ ◆ ◆

We're not quite done. There's still a collection of symptoms to look at that fall freely into what I call the "Free Fallin'" category.

FREE FALLIN'

Besides the primary symptoms discussed so far, there are a handful of other behaviors considered to be traits of BPD. None of them will get an entire chapter of their own here, but they are still important to know about.

Emptiness

The emptiness a BP feels is far more profound than what you and I experience. While we can hopefully convince ourselves that our feelings of emptiness are temporary, and therefore manageable, the BP considers them hopeless and infinite. In all-or-nothing fashion, they have a nearly impossible time seeing beyond the gloom until their mood swings the other way.

Mistrust

As you can imagine, if your spouse is constantly terrified of abandonment, they may not be able trust you. Trying to tell a BP that you love them is like quenching their thirst with an eyedropper. The moment you give them a drop, they immediately crave more. When you balk at delivering an endless supply, they mistrust your motives and attack you.

Interpersonal Sensitivity

Many BPs have the ability to quickly assess personality keystones in others and make use of the information to get what they need. This is extremely helpful in the workplace and allows BPs to succeed and be well liked in their profession.

Control Issues

Often feeling helpless and without self-identity, a BP might overcompensate by aggressively trying to control people and situations around them. Following in the symptom of "extremes," the BP will see their world as either right or wrong. Everything is either in its place (on time, on budget, picture perfect, etc.), or it is wrong. Taking control allows them to maintain order.

Situational Competence

While their personal relationships are often a cesspool of disaster, the BP may be highly successful in other areas. This is likely the case at school, work, athletics, or a serious hobby.

In this regard, the BP is taking control issues and focusing them on being productive. If you want a project done on time and nearly perfect, put a Borderline on the job.

Impaired self-direction

Conversely, a BP may enter phases where their life shatters and nothing gets accomplished. They ask, "How can I think about finding a job when I'm not even sure I exist?" The feelings of emptiness and despair take over and can't be overridden.

Eventually, their mood swings the other direction and a phase of positive-minded productivity begins again.

No Object Constancy

Earlier, I talked about how babies can't conceive of a thing's existence if it is not within their range of senses. If they don't hear, see, taste, smell, or feel mom, she's no longer in the same realm.

As adults, we have developed the skills to handle the absence of someone we care about. We miss them dearly, but understand that over time, the feeling will recede. Not so the BP.

To them, they still cling to their infant-like belief that an object is not constant. If they can't keep it in the room, it's never coming back. Imagine how terrifying life is for your spouse suffering from those feelings *every time* you step out the door.

Narcissistic Demands

I have read that about 25% of BPs also have narcissistic personality disorder. The narcissist is known for constantly drawing attention back to themselves, especially in public.

Like a child throwing a tantrum, a BP will act out in movie theaters, stores, amusement parks, and church. They will want others to see and verify that you aren't being a loving and supportive spouse. If outsiders take their side, it fuels their belief that says, "I'm not the crazy one. *You* are."

Boundaries

Try setting a personal boundary with a BP and you will rapidly learn how much they don't like such things. Sentences that include "but" are a common trigger. "I love you, but..." "I know you'd like me to stay, but..." "This may feel acceptable to you, but..." All of these statements set boundaries. They draw lines that society says will activate consequences if you cross them.

In the all-or-nothing, right-or-wrong world of the BP, boundaries are meant to be blasted asunder in a fiery rage.

◆ ◆ ◆

Now that you've reviewed the symptoms of BPD, I bet you understand much more about the turmoil in your marriage. The bizarre, random behavior is starting to make sense. In fact, it has a name—borderline personality disorder.

Do you feel convinced your spouse has BPD?

Do you want more information?

Would you like suggestions to reclaim your self-respect and make your life easier?

Turn the page.

EMPTY SPACES

This book is meant as a down and dirty "street-guide" to BPD and its symptoms. Now that you know the basics, you may desire additional "real-life" information to fill the empty spaces.

To learn more about challenges others like you have experienced and if solutions are available, I have other fully loaded books you'll want to check out. To visit my Amazon author page and find more BPD titles, simply scan this QR code into your phone or device:

Specific titles you should look into include:

BDP from the Husband's POV: *The Roses and Rage of My Wife's Borderline Personality Disorder*

Written *by* a husband of a Borderline *for* husbands of Borderlines. A gripping and sometimes cringe-inducing exposé of loving someone with a personality disorder. In a non-clinical and stunning first-person account, Robert Page delivers "What I wish I had done" insight and optimism to others on the same path. Book #2 in the *Roses to Rage BPD* series.

Married to Borderline Personality Disorder: *Your BPD Stories of Roses and Rage*

The only BPD book of its kind! Focused entirely on accounts shared by readers who have faced head-on living with a BP marriage. Learn from others who have already "been there—done that" presented in non-clinical and compassionate language. Book #3 in the *Roses to Rage BPD* series.

I've Written My Story; Now You Tell Me Yours

Join the Facebook support group, Roses and Rage: Spouses of Borderline Personality Disorder, to share your experiences. I would especially love to hear from spouses who have found ways to reduce the BPD problems in your relationship.

Pass It On!

If you enjoyed this "short-read" book and found it useful, I'd be very grateful if you'd **post an honest review** at the Amazon website. The more reviews, the higher the chances that others who need the book will see it.

To leave a review, all you need to do is visit the book's Amazon page. While you're at the page, please "follow" me as an author so you'll be notified about future books.

Thank you for the support,
~Robert

OTHER RESOURCES

I am only presenting here resources that I have personally reviewed and found useful. Perhaps they will be helpful to you as well.

25 Songs That Describe the 9 Classic Symptoms of Borderline Personality Disorder. 2018. *The Mighty* (blog) at https://themighty.com/2018/07/borderline-personality-disorder-songs-symptoms/

Arabi, Shahida. 2016. *Becoming the Narcissist's Nightmare: How to Devalue and Discard the Narcissist While Supplying Yourself.* CreateSpace Independent Publishing.

Borderline personality disorder. 2019. Article available online from the Mayo Clinic.

Borderline Personality Disorder. Article from the National Alliance on Mental Illness. https://www.nami.org/Learn-More/Mental-Health-Conditions/Borderline-Personality-Disorder

Borderline Personality Disorder. Undated public-domain pamphlet available from the National Institute of Mental Health.

DSM-IV and DSM-5 Criteria for the Personality Disorders. 2012. American Psychiatric Association.

Eddy, Bill. 2011. *Splitting: Protecting Yourself While Divorcing Someone with Borderline or Narcissistic Personality Disorder.* New Harbinger Publications.

Fjelstad, Margalis. 2014. *Stop Caretaking the Borderline or Narcissist: How to End the Drama and Get On with Life.* Rl Publishing.

Kreisman, Jerold, MD and Hal Straus. 2010. *I Hate You—Don't Leave Me: Understanding the Borderline Personality*. New York: Penguin Group.

Johnson, Merri Lisa. 2010. *Girl in Need of a Tourniquet: Memoir of a Borderline Personality.* Berkeley, CA: Seal Press.

Linehan, Marsha M. 2014. *DBT Training Skills Manuel*, 2nd ed. The Guilford Press.

Mason, Paul, MS and Randi Kreger. 2010. *Stop Walking on Eggshells: Taking Your Life Back When Someone You Care About Has Borderline Personality Disorder,* 2nd *ed.* Oakland, CA: New Harbinger Publications, Inc.

Stout, Martha. 2006. *The Sociopath Next Door*. Harmony Publishing.

ABOUT THE AUTHOR

Robert Page is a pen name. I hold a doctorate degree from a fully accredited state university and have published several #1 Amazon best-sellers in non-fiction. After a decade in academia, I returned to my home-state roots to work in a "dream job" with the support of my wife and family. Under my real name, I have written various accounts of my experience with BPD, but the details in this book are so revealing that it would be inappropriate for me to risk the anonymity of others against their wishes. Therefore, all the names (including the pets) and locations have been changed. Please follow my Amazon Author page for more information.